Dear Rev.
David Kasbow

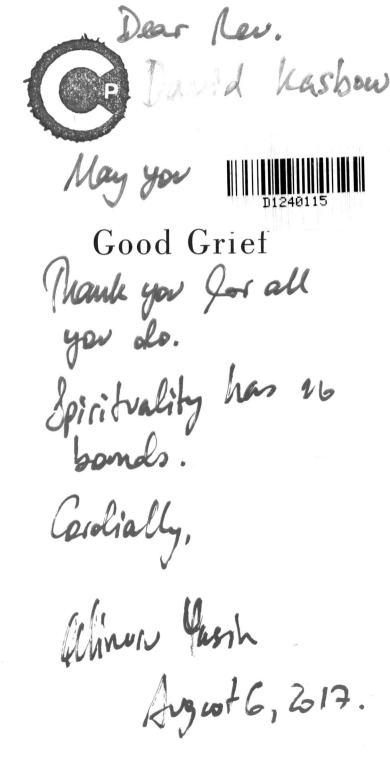

May you

D1240115

Good Grief

Thank you for all
you do.

Spirituality has no
bonds.

Cordially,

Alinor Yassih

August 6, 2017.

Good Grief

60 Days
with 60 Poems

ALINURU YASIN

Published by Coconut Publications, Inc., Auburn Hills, MI
www.alinuru.com

Edited and Designed by Girl Friday Productions
www.girlfridayproductions.com
Editorial: Nicole Burns-Ascue
Interior Design: Rachel Christenson
Cover Design: David Drummond

ISBN (Paperback): 978-1-945823-98-5
e-ISBN: 978-1-945823-96-1

Library of Congress Control Number: 2017940123

First Edition

Printed in the United States of America

In memory of
Mimi and loved ones
who
generously and ardently aspired to unconditional love.

Preface

Read, learn, read . . .
The one not taught . . . is schooled by the Universe . . . ,
For (the benefit of) our children's children,
Embodied with our culture,
Filled with our happiness,
Our unyielding love,
Altogether with our blessings.

February 17, 2016

Author's Note

Sixty days ago, Mr. and Mrs. Death invaded my home; sixty days ago, my world turned upside down; our plans in vain, not the Lord's plans, clearly. I had no choice; I had to do what I had to do.

My family, friends, and colleagues have helped me tremendously. You did have a choice, and you chose to care for me in your own special, unique ways. As I faced the abyss of death and grief, I was ready to plunge deep down and rid myself of life, a life that panged me, a life riddled with deep pain and sorrow. I would have gone to great lengths without your comfort and support and, most important, your genuine love. With the help of grace, more love, companionship, and friendship, I managed to get through every day. I kept saying, "We're made out of tough stuff" and "Life is full of surprises." It is and we are. You supported my listing soul; you courageously pulled me away from the edge of the abyss. You brought me back to a safe harbor. You nurtured me and consoled me. You listened to me and kept me on this side of the light.

My account is in deficit, my account balance negative. However, my account balance is approaching zero and turning into a positive number. I can feel it; I know it; I am very optimistic about a future that offers me nothing but hope, faith, and a journey filled with joy and discovery. There is something moving inside of me like an avalanche. The scaffolding of my dam is still there, and that reservoir will be full soon. When the next floodwaters arrive, I will hold firm and stand strong and tall. I plan to release my effort, my energy, in a controlled manner; a release that is purposefully achieved so that I, too, may help you, you, and you. Very soon, I, too, will be helpful and offer my hand in assistance, my arm as support, and my shoulders for stability.

Moreover, I look forward to sharing what I have learned in my short life with you. These sixty days have gone by so fast. I look forward to another sixty and, perhaps, a thousand more. I want my 1,001 Arabian Nights; I need my eighty weeks around the world. Has my time come? Well, one can never be certain, with Mr. and Mrs. Death lurking.

Let us begin with every day we have and make the most of it. Thank you from the very bottom of my empty heart. I will never repine about life again, for we have *Sixty Days with Sixty Poems*. Hopefulness transcends us all.

May we have the joy of seeing each other and know that we wish one another the very best in this life and all that it has to offer. Carpe diem.

Alinuru M. Yasin
April 7, 2016

Herculean Triumphant—The Champ

I,
Am,
Ali,
Cassius Clay,
And his becoming,
Muhammad Ali became,
I floated like a butterfly and stung like a bee,
Left right jab, uppercut jazz, fight like you mean it, a raging
bull in the tight planet,
Is right mighty? I stood all alone, then support came along,
I stood tall, I said no, I found good help along the way, and
they all came my way,
Left hook knockout, right on the rope, in the rumble of
the jungle down with Manila thriller, I could have become a
killer but chose peace,
Peace, peace, peace, justice for all, we are all equal in the eyes
of the benevolent,
We are all the same with a purpose; seek, yearn for it,
Become who you are meant to be,
Muhammad Ali,
Shall always,
Guide us,
Champ,
Me.

After April 17, 2016, when I completed the sixty poems, I could not write anything. I was numb and somber. More or less, I sent out the weekly e-mails to family and friends and continued with life: an exercise routine whereby I have been running and practicing yoga. The new vigorous routine allowed me to lose over fifty pounds. Then, with the passing of the Champ, something began to move inside me. Dare I say: a rumble, a new beginning to connect with others who have lost and worked through their grief?

A tribute to a beacon of hope and equality for all, a person who opened doors for many, and a pillar that has supported many, allowing them to rise up with respect, diligence, and twinkles in their eyes. For Mr. Jon B., thank you for sharing your personal encounters with a legend.

Moreover, on June 26, 2016, while visiting my sister and my delightful niece, I watched the children play. I witnessed the children celebrating my niece's sixth birthday. My hands moved quickly toward paper as I began to write a new series of poems under the working title *Hopefulness in the Ordinary*. The birthday poem is the first of many more to come. Our intersecting, intermingling, and engaging extraordinary lives are a precious daily gift.

Good Grief

60. Blessings for Tomorrow: Good Grief . . .

When there is a beginning, there is an end.
Igneous, sedimentary, metamorphic,
Birth, marriage, death,
They come in threes,
Even the three wise men.

We know we are just passing through,
A transit of the soul,
A physical manifestation of Our Dear Lord,
A unique part of the universe.

We laugh, we smile, we cry, we mourn,
We share, we love, we fear, we adorn,
We whisper, we shout, we cherish, we lose,
It's the moments that count, not the excuses.

Verily life is a precious gift,
With a blink or snap it is gone,
With the raging illness it is cruelly prolonged,
How do we fit together the pieces of the puzzle?

Can we? Can't we? Should we? Shouldn't we?
Figure it out. What's the purpose? What's the secret?
Figure it out. Good grief, the void.
Good grief, I miss her, good grief, I miss him.
Good grief, we miss them.

On days like these when a loved one has passed on,
Remember to stop and count our blessings,
Take stock of the good things,
Take pride in all those we have helped and encountered.

Keep the end in sight as the final stage is old age,
At times a useful lie is better than a useless fact,
It may not be, it's touch and go,
We each have a load to bear, one step at a time.

Take a moment to self-examine,
Do we owe anyone an apology? Do we need to reach out?
Helping another by being there, being present,
Linger and stay a bit longer.

Clear our minds of the nonsense chatter,
None of those nagging things matter,
Listen with our ears, listen with our hearts,
Audaciously, listen with our bodies.

It may be tomorrow. Tomorrow never comes . . .
Good grief, good grief, good grief,
They come in three of a kind,
The wheels of the world continue to turn and churn.
May our loved ones be blessed and rest in peace.

April 3, 2016

59. On the Brink

Pay attention: all races end at the corner . . .
Over there? Over here? Just there?
So sorry, I do not understand.
Tell me again, wait a moment, let's repeat it again.

What did you say? Did you mean this or that?
Now we understand each other completely,
Truthfully, equally, amicably.
Just a moment, let me write it down for future reference.

So here's what happened:
I got hit. Yes, I was minding my own business,
I got hit. I was in my own world,
I got hit. Yes, I was in the zone,
I got hit. No, I was not paying attention.

On my phone, in the zone,
Well, my smartphone is an extension of me,
Looking down, looking away, not paying attention,
Oblivious as I may be, let's just rationalize,
They will look out for me, right?

The rules are not meant for me,
No, no, they do not apply,
Societal safety nets, the entitlement, the chatter, the pain,
The lack of aptitude, the lack of properness.
It's not okay, pay attention!

In comparison, are you hit more or less of the time?
The human nature to be right all the time,
What is the right cost? What was the intention?
The road to hell is paved with good intentions,
The momentum will roll you that way with a purpose.

A misguided direction with weight will grow,
Just like the snowball that grows bigger and bigger,
It will grow out of control,
Unless, of course, we start to pay attention,
Offer no harm to others in order to preserve ourselves.

Let's do the right thing,
Live without a shred of doubt,
Let's make sure every day is a gift to overcome the trial,
Embrace the lesson, recognize the opportunity,
Overcome the challenge, beat the threat, and thrive, not just
    survive.

April 2, 2016

58. Work

Attitudes matter,
Work is work is work,
Whether one is a bus driver, teacher, lawyer, or barber.

It's a balancing act,
Give and take, ebb and flow,
Some days are great, others are slow,
Divinely know others are just too low.

Decide to be helpful to others,
More will come during the day,
Every day's goal is to do our best,
Take only what you can do,
Let the rest go by and by,
To ensure peace of mind.

Work is not given on silver salver,
Purposefully align value,
Join a team that races to the finish,
Fostering and remembering joy,
Watching, learning, and growing.

If there is a beginning there is an ending,
In the end what truly matters is getting through the day,
With a smile on your face,
With the paycheck,
That's never enough,
Surely, it is what it is.

Our efforts are not in vain,
The choice is ours to show,
For we have more than we know,
Committing and focusing diligently.

It's a strategy to show more,
Via the other eight hours is not a chore,
Wishfully, they are ours free and clear to roar . . .

February 25, 2016

57. Life's Sojourner

Safari,
Let's do it, we should dream big, let's do it. Really, really?
We make plans, we redo the plans,
Some get done, others undone—no care nor muster.

Oh, yes, I know what I need: NC-28,
That mountainous North Carolina Dragon's Tail road.
Bring me the open road; give me the twists and turns,
The dips with hairpin loops . . .

With lead foot and downshifting clutch foot,
The worldly breathtaking views open with the high road,
The cool shaded eyes stay put.
Great cheer is felt here as the asphalt licks away . . .

Lucky devil, it's measured due is given . . .
For living is a quarter mile at a time,
Dashing toward destiny, burning toward the goal,
The insides are churning: bring me the open road . . .

Thrilling with the plan, the gloves firmly encase the hands,
Yet the unraveling experience is much more than getting
    there,
Enjoy every turn, every sight. Engage completely.
No distractions because one never knows . . .
The last quarter mile may be just yonder,
Submerse immensely before we ponder.
Savor the moment, sip it in,
After all we're going for a spin.

When we look back five, ten, fifteen years or more,
Can we honestly say: "We lived life to the fullest"?
The stellar road from Cape Town to Cairo is incomplete,
The Paris-Dakar Rally is not replete.

Implementation is a no go,
Let's make a crew: "Come on, Skip, and you . . ."
"We talked, we dreamed, what's stopping us now?"
Stop! Ahh yes, life's commitments and obligations.
No regrets: that will be the day to have just the drive,
How about the Blue Ridge Parkway?
Or the Pacific Coast Highway?
Did we give up on our dreams? Wondering why . . .

Flats, detours, speed bumps, closures, and barrels . . .
Of course, there's much more . . .
But you know what: thanks to you, and you, and you,
No regrets. I'm living in my dreams a quarter mile at a time.

April 2, 2016

56. Relationships of Birds and Bees

Yes, birds do it and bees do it—we all do it,
Yes, they even leave their parents' nest and hive behind,
Yes, they coordinate and work together in the rearing,
Knowing when the time comes, they all leave for a new life.

The choice is obvious: batten down the hatches,
Eat, sleep, eat, sleep, feed, sleep, feed,
Or not, is there more to the rearing?
Warden, demigod, or cicerone? A friendly guide, not augurs.

The lazy choice may well be,
Labor Absent Zero Yield,
But the busy-ness prevails,
We have to do this and that for the little ones.

The million mash prayers do get answered,
The million gestures of effort do get replied to,
The million deign, and touches do come through,
A million times and more, they will still leave you.

Life is fleeting, life is moving, life is gleaning,
Jettisoned hie, they have their own life, their own destiny,
At their zenith, they will make their own milieu,
They will make their own way as soon as the wings open up.

The birds know it, and so do the bees,
New beginnings, new destinations, new flowers to keep,
Home is home, but once we leave,

We can never go back home in that sense anyway.

The wheels of life churn and chew us up,
The protection of the homey nest is gone,
It's up to us to shape up and step up,
Flutter those wings and soar, crank out the effort and buzz.

Some days it's a good day to be a bird,
After a soaking rain, the worms are up to play,
The birds feast to their gullets on easy pickings,
Thank goodness for a rainy day, yum, yum.

Other days, it's good to be a bee,
Just buzz and bee,
They gather the pollen, feed each other,
Keep us healthy with honey, keep us fed with their efforts.

Luck is a good,
Love unconditionally with courtesy and kindness,
Then, labor under the common knowledge:
The harder one works, the luckier one gets . . .

So where do we draw the line and come to terms,
Can we quietly coexist? Parents and children,
We perform a sacred duty, a delicate survival and balance,
By and by, we could die without the birds and the bees.

April 2, 2016

55. Understanding

It's more than permeability, pore pressure,
More than the movements of water through sheer pressure,
It's more than what was said or done,
It is truthfulness.

Our thick skulls protect the water inside,
With the conduit-sealed entrance so well designed,
The eyes see, the ears hear,
The nose smells, the skin senses,
Each report: garbage in garbage out. Are we truthful to
    ourselves?

Is it too much effort to delve deeper before the mouth and
    tongue jabber?
Yes, we're all up for a good chin-wag,
Spew, spew, spew, is it really necessary?
What happened to the train of thought stopping at the
    check station?
If we have nothing pleasant to say, it's best we remain silent.

Silence never betrays,
Silence is the best defense as in "I'm taking the Fifth,"
Silence as in "Zen, I'm self-reflecting,"
"Quit badgering me, my opinions don't matter,
My thoughts are my own."

Let me be, go away!
If you keep at it, I will have a pyrrhic eruption,

My tectonic skull may mangle yours and it will be
    unpleasant,
Let me be,
Give me space.

They say time heals all wounds?
What wounds? Who's they? And who said anything about
    healing?
Seek to understand before giving advice,
The pressure and heat is too much,
Perhaps relief will come in time, but just not now.

Unfortunately, by then, in good time, we will have changed,
Metamorphosized into something completely
    unrecognizable,
We're in the trenches, in the badlands,
Perhaps a different time, a different place, a different
    outlook,
Will we be crystallized or fossilized? Change is inevitable.

Let's just be quiet about it,
Let's coexist, you go your way and I will go mine,
You do your thing and I will do mine,
Let's agree to disagree,
And understand peaceful coexistence.

March 31, 2016

54. Stars: Avoiding Ugliness

A sense of direction, Deneb within Cygnus, or pulsing Vega,
The northern stars are eternal with sidereal time,
It's relative but always on the move, always there,
We just have to see and follow the signs,
The Northern Cross blazes as a guide ahead.

The bird has left the bird's nest, and many more mammoth
  structures,
These buildings are living, breathing beauties,
They suck and bellow, they heave and totter,
Imaginations and dreams of a wonder, a thoughtful spirit.

The bird has left the bird's nest,
But we will always remember your style, your flair,
Your elegance, your determination,
Your passion, your gusto, your instructions and mentorship.

Sharpen the pencil, draw the lines,
Chisel those draft lines until the parchment sings,
Calculate the dimensions, balance it with taste,
Work within the processes and systems.

Now test the boundaries. Team, these are not my schematics,
Back to work, let's start over. That's not what I designed,
This is not nomadic, it is principally symbolic,
Expressing our thoughts to stand the test of time.

Yes, it's not the pyramids nor the vitality of the Louvre,
But an ever-present, unavoidable art with a function,
The function must be balanced with materials, beauty,
Pragmatism, utility, experience, and societal symbolism.

The end product is a timeless satisfaction,
The interwoven spaces offer delight, perception, molding,
The buildings will shape us,
Scale and proportion are balanced with pi.

Color and lighting glimmer,
Subtle hues and textures are for a distinguished class,
Ugliness to be avoided at all cost,
Breathe and believe in the rococo rhythm,
It will stand the test of time.

April 2, 2016

53. On the Train

Chooo, choooo; we're on the move,
Tickets, please,
All aboard!
Time to feel time,
Cha cha cha cha chaaa . . .

Acres of fields in my mind,
Keep your view far and wide,
Acres of mind in those fields,
Fields that keep secrets firmly,
The economist . . . I always remember him on trains.

The grass sways in the wind, side to side,
Just like loose change,
These tracks are like neurons, far from foreign,
Intertwined, linked, and fully engaged,
Nostalgia and fingerswiping.

But moving forward toward unbelievable events,
Track change, keep that attention span, though!
Which way to living in our dreams?
Embrace the past; where's my coffee?
Right here, do you have everything you need?

Seven quarters, how many left? Ah, time,
Great . . . enjoy,
Clapham minutes away, then Waterloo,
Home sweet home,

Waterloo that side, hug.

Do you remember our first encounter?
Waterloo in my darting eyes,
It's a forever thing,
Yes, a single moment crystallized,
Well done.

March 14, 2016

52. Fluidity: Clinton River Tales

Universal values and democracy at work,
Where to begin? The promises?
The camaraderie, the handshakes, or the good wishes?
Aren't we better off? What's on the agenda? What are the
   plans?

Will we get blasted, cruised, or trumped? Who knows?
A good message: makeup, setup, move up,
Begin the debates, ditch the talking points, exchange the blows,
Pound the thunderous drums as the humdrum builds up.

Messages roll over beyond normal proportions,
Escalate into a quadrillion delicious portions,
Agreements gravely made with confirmed heels,
Let's keep moving, let's retain ideals.

Values and codes of conduct may prevail.
Elbow grease, voter support, voter turnout,
Defining and overcoming a nation's glaring issues wail,
It can be done. Let's keep it moving, no burnout.

Let's enjoy the game by engaging the mind,
Let's review the facts and never be led blind,
Through open debates and collaboration,
With healthy competition for the duration.

By and by, we're living in history,
Momenta, we're twirling through space,

Stars aligned with sidereal time never lie, a revealing
    mystery!
It's in the galactic system, it's more than being an ace.

It's like ironing a white shirt while watching the wrinkles
Disappear with a twinkle,
The initial position is crisp, withering away like time,
Fading away, only to be worn and soiled with grime.

Curious at all levels for our own mental health,
Freedom questions power, status checks wealth,
Time stealthily tells and wins,
Will the end justify the means? Time always grins . . .

March 31, 2016

51. Reflecting on Expectations

We specialize in the impossible,
Reflect on what motivates us,
Is it the high tide of ignorance? That loud, strong, worri-
    some bully,
Delivering misconceptions like a tsunami, suddenly
    devastating,
While temporary, it's here, then gone just like a season.

Perhaps the gruesome aftermath and recovery may be
    avoided,
So be prepared, be on the ready, parry away, and stand
    guard,
Armed with knowledge and wisdom,
Let's prevail just as the mighty white cliffs bluff the tides
    below,
The lighthouse is here to stay, piercing through cloudy
    storms,
The shining beacon of light guides and warns.

So keep the faith, be carefree once in a while,
Believe to achieve with rolling knowledge and churning
    wisdom,
Sharing our truth, uniting in the good,
By weeding and keeping that tedious ignorance at bay,
Enlightening and becoming, we pray.

Shining is the sun on every cloudy day,
Yet we fail to see; at times, we fail to believe,

Seeing is believing; that's easier said than done,
Leaping with blind faith is a true calling,
Exploring is not boring.

Let us examine the truth, weed out the ignorance,
Let us rely on our instincts to become and overcome,
Let us soar above the folly,
Let us stand and be jolly,
Unlearn the folly and relearn the jolly.

We have the capacity to exceed insurmountable obstacles,
Tenuous situations, outsmart the impossible because it's all
    relative,
Let's choose wisely,
For the better, with the light,
We can make it right.

April 2, 2016

50. Zero Little Big

Are you the little person or the big person?
Either way do not forget the little person, big person,
When things turn better, bigger person,
You say, "No, no, never!"

Aren't you standing on the shoulders of the little person?
Bigger person, you placate and favor,
Surely are you treating people well?
The little person is as essential as a building block.

Just like the cute burrowing muskrat,
That made its home in a levee,
The multimillion-dollar levee collapsed during the flood,
The little people were affected.

The bigger people never got the blame,
Never got hurt because they lived way away from such perils,
Is right might? Or is might right?
The ethics of the matter will not prevail.

We cannot delve into the nitty-gritty,
Big people do not have the time to be bothered,
Little people just try to get by with time,
Are our core values different?

Our beliefs, our religions, our organizations, our businesses,
The little people, the big people,
The folding and unfolding, the Yin and Yang,

The balance of integrity, faithfulness, privacy, and fairness.

Is it safe? Do we have the support? Keep flipping that coin,
How many sides to a coin? Yes, heads. No, tails.
How about the rambling, rolling side?
The coin will roll away and land elsewhere.

Nowhere, now here, a new journey has begun,
Keep on flipping, keep on trekking, keep on doing,
Little person is the same as the big person,
We are all equal in the universal eye.

Yet, in the nameless, faceless societal eye we are different,
Them, us; those, theirs; yours, ours; yours, mine,
Yes, the cautious seldom err,
But big people are trampling over the little people.

Their sights are farther out of the woods, not squarely on
    the trees,
Little people can broaden their horizons, their sights, by
    taking the elevator,
Up, up, away, it will cost ya . . . unless we learn to soar,
Let's keep up the reading, let's keep trekking, let's keep on
    doing.

Big people and little people can work together,
It takes one to reach and teach one, it makes one to be one,
One by one, let's move on up,
Let's better one another through democracy.

March 31, 2016

49. What's on Your Mind?

Post . . . Like . . . Share . . . Repeat . . .

Are you kidding me?
How dare you ask the question? Don't you know I'm
      grieving!
Well, maybe not; because it's a good open-ended question,
Let me think. Huh . . .

You are making me think and share! Okay.
You are smart, and your affluence reflects that. Good.
Respect, flattery, insight, good wishes,
Are all for you.

But back to me,
The challenge is my responsibility,
I will try my very best to be lucky,
Labor under common knowledge, yes!

And maybe, just maybe,
I will also make something out of nothing,
Back to work,
I'm thinking, I'm thinking, I'm thinking.

I'm working, I'm working, I'm working,
The best part: the harder I work, the luckier I get,
Thanks for the impromptu,
Oh, and I shared.

More to come. Peaceful goodness.

February 28, 2016

48. Entrapment Spiral

Be strong, be brave, sort out your problems,
Fight the crave, fight the itch, creeper,
Harness yourself to fix the glitch.
Yes, things may have happened to you in the past,
But hold on to your own filth, smudge no more,
And do not relay the baton to the next generation.

End the cycle of poison, deceit, and victimhood,
Rise above your own weaknesses,
Do not allow yourself to wallow in self-pity and spite,
Things that were done to you are inexcusable,
Incomprehensible, undeniably vile,
But stop. Please stop the hateful cycle.

Look toward the light, get the help you need,
So that you may do right, no wishy-washy stuff,
Be strong, be firm, be unyielding to the cracked vessel
    within,
That hole inside will never get filled,
The void is permanently there, it's yours to keep,
Speak up and share your pain with trusted ones.

Just like Humpty Dumpty could not be put back together
    again,
Lessen your burden by writing and sharing your plight,
Why in the world would someone else afflict you with pain,
An innocent one, yes you were, dealt a severe blow,
Pull yourself up by your bootstraps, rise, rise, rise above.

Break it down . . . Better to overcome half the fear, than the
    whole . . .

Linger a bit, wallow some more,
But above all,
Say and do no more harm to others,
Recall the Golden Rule,
Although it did not apply to you,
Please, please, rise above, let the future be harmed no more.

March 24, 2016

47. Treasured Affectionate Terms

Our pets are our source of unconditional love,
When introduced at the young, tender age,
Of innocence and playfulness,
They become too close to our hearts.

When does all this closeness change?
No more cute names?
No more endearing terms?
How did we lose track and get so far away?

Kiwi, Mocha, Tingaling, Dior, Dora, Trevor,
Samson, Moulan, Annabelle, Lucy, Priscilla,
Pearl, Ryley, Nova, Peaches, Coco, Chase,
Sparkles, Baby Cakes, Kobe, Enzo, Paisley.

Brody, Juju, Momo, CJ, Winnie, Bradaigh,
Jazzy, Hattie, Firecracker, Arrow, Canon,
Itsy, Bitsy, Crunch, Inky, Chloe, Dodo,
Gracie, Emmie, Rachele, Jet, Classy Luke.

Cookie, Shadow, Bella, Precious, Cali, Canna,
Gorgeous, Ms. Kitty, Atticus, Lulu, Bullit,
Dumbo, Frizzy, Buddy, Sport, Milo, Fifi,
Bentley, Ella, Frannie, Elf, Harley, Xsar, Missy . . .

Can't we just hold on to them a little bit longer?
We never want to let go
Of the fondly stored memories,

By keeping them closer.

Love never dies . . . Sometimes it fades and tarnishes.
Embellish the tale; share the chuckle, even just a knuckle,
Our pets cherished without truckle,
Heartily within us they are . . . Always: now and forever . . .

February 25, 2016

46. My Nutty Uncle

"Which size, Uncle?
Do you need a wrench, too?
Sure, I'm your gofer,
And I'm learning, too."

"Not this kind?
Okay, please tell me a story,
Dear Uncle."

"Well, nuts come in all shapes and sizes,
We have the metal kind and the tasty kind,
Mmm, there's another kind, too.

"Peanuts, walnuts, pistachio nuts, Brazil nuts,
Almonds, coconuts, cashews, macadamia nuts,
Technically, some are seeds, but hey.
If you call a nut a nut,
Like Dusty and Lefty,
Or like Rusty and Empty.

"You'll come across the good nuts and the bad,
The trick is to separate them,
Just like people, some are helpful,
Others not so much,
Just like products, good ones outsell,
Bad ones have to be sold.

"The sooner you know, the better you are

At keeping a wide berth to steer clear,
Of the riffraff you should never be near.

"You're too young to know we're a whole buncha nuts,
It's too early to think: Ugo, Ugo, Cha, Cha, Cha . . .
So, stop slacking, back to work,
And bring me some nuts."

February 28, 2016

45. The Way Forward

My hero and champion says, "Ever forward, never
    backward,"
A pioneer, a forward thinker, a tinkerer, an integrator,
Who's self-reliant, felicitous, and even defiant?

Ever forward, never backward,
What's in the past is in the past,
Take the detour, take the side road,
Explore toward wonderland . . .

Embrace the rhythm of life as we glide through space,
We are moving with and amongst the stars,
We are standing on the shoulders of giants,
We're soaring at considerable levels and beyond description.

We have the ability to move mountains, to fly to the moon,
And the ability to focus on the things that matter,
The common things are much more similar,
Far from being too different.

The mother's embrace,
The father's sensibility,
A sibling's rivalrous taunt,
A friend's support and companionship.

A spouse's unyielding and undying love,
A life partner's dreams and desires,
A teacher's lifelong guidance and instruction,

A mentor's gift of sharing.

We harbor and carry these traits,
They are within us as a means to live forward,
Ever forward,
And never backward.

April 3, 2016

44. The Secret of Victoria's Closet

Yes, the clothes make the lady,
No, the man is self-made and clothes help,
If God intended for one style,
We would not have been born naked, vulnerable, and fragile.

Clothes, clothes, clothes,
Really, life is too short to wear boring clothes,
But as we all know,
The Emperor should always wear clothes,
The Empress leaves much to desire.

The texture, the touch, the feel, the fit, the color,
It's the clothes that make us feel present,
It's the clothes that make or break us,
Before we even open our mouths.

Yes, what's inside matters,
No, we won't get a chance to express what's inside,
If our outside doesn't shatter the interest of another,
Or fails to sparkle the things that may be,
Or twinkle the hope of what can be.

The story of what you were up to,
The tale of the treasure hunting,
The history of that scarf, that sweater, this blouse,
Those pants and stockings, this evening dress, that coat.

So go ahead: you see it, you want it, you just charge it,

Forget about your husband's glare,
He thinks he's the warden, but he's not!
He just doesn't know what clothes do for you . . .
You are divine, unique, and special: Express yourself well!

March 19, 2016

43. Nourishing Hair Therapy

An everchanging art and style,
The eye is on the mark,
She tells you which style she wants,
Listen closely, pay attention.

Her hair is dynamic, it flows in the wind,
It shines in the sun with a patina,
Pay attention, she's trusting you,
Be smart, be attentive.

Yes, styles change, seasons change,
It's a different season, and she wants to feel special,
Deliver, provide,
By and by, consistent she is.

The hair unloading is not all she leaves,
Indeed, it is gossip we routinely crave,
Our deepest and darkest secrets of love and hate,
So easily revealed as the snip-snip goes.

The next time I see her,
Her personality, her lifestyle, her stories,
Will be more as she interacts with the world,
It's not just her hair.

It's attitude, it's grace, it's the look, it's the feel,
She is special, she is unique, and she needs me,
Curly, wavy, or straight,

It needs to fit her face, her personality, and her flair.
More than the highlights and the lowlights,
More than the brushing, the cutting, the trimming,
Much, much, more than the blow-drying or flatironing thy
    hair.

To be my best, and when I deliver,
She will feel great as she is radiant,
She walks with a lift
In her upbeat mood and spirit.

"Yes," says the mirror on the wall,
"Consistently, it takes character to speak the truth
    always . . ."
After she's done with me,
The mirror will also say: "Honey dear, you look great!"

March 2, 2016

42. Rejuvenation at Hatcher's Waterfalls

It's on a private byway, no trespassing,
The water rushes by and by,
Two of a kind: rock and water.

The rock says, "I won't budge."
The water replies, "No, no, not today.
But I will tickle you, caress you,
And make such a noise,
I will not be ignored.

"In time, I will wear you down,
Then, when we get together,
We shall push you, we shall move you,
Just as easy as a feather in the wind,
We are patient, we will circle back.
We will slow down to a trickle,
And then, we will rise back.

"Dearest rock,
You are stuck in one place,
One moment, one time zone,
No, no, not us, we get around,
We move about and we will move you,
Now or later, we will whisk you,
Whether you like it or not.

"We are water, the bringers of life,
The fluid that joins all creatures together,

We are life.
We give and we take,
We break and we make.

"Let's enjoy our time together,
Let's enjoy this time,
Because in the end: you will break."

March 19, 2016

41. Faith in Comfy Food

The aroma makes my mouth water,
The desire gives me the quivers,
The oven is warm and ready,
The batter is airy and tasty.

We're in the zone.
The temperature is right,
The timer is set,
Bake and poof, voilà!

Here comes the blueberry muffin,
Here are the madeleines,
Here are the wants . . . no, no . . . our needs!
A friend in need is a friend in deed . . .

It's the hint of a familiar taste,
The licking of the fork,
The last nibble off the spoon.

The simple touch with our fingers.
I take you, I pick you,
I lick you, I devour you,
Inside and out, feeling the food go deep down . . .

Let's enjoy happiness,
With the sensations and familiarity,
Just like Grandma and Grandpa as they spoil us:
With loving gestures; with generous portions.

His ease in changing subjects,
Her effortlessness in serving coffee, tea, or lemonade,
With everlasting love,
That's faith in comfy food feeding our souls.

March 14, 2016

40. Milk and Lakes

In the beginning it is milk that instills and nurtures,
In the beginning it is milk the nourishes and protects,
In the beginning it is milk that defends,
Silence never betrays.

Victoria, Tanganyika, Nyasa.
Victoria is sweet, Tanganyika is long, Nyasa is short.

In the beginning it is clean freshwater,
In the beginning it is the glaciers that scrounge and retain,
In the beginning it is the fault lines that give way,
Baikal, Superior, Michigan, Huron, Erie, Ontario.

Baikal the deep, Superior the cold, Michigan the barrier,
Huron the connector, Erie the linking, Ontario the director.

Still waters run thunderously deep.

In the end will we outgrow the taste,
In the end will we squander the resource,
In the end will we preserve milk and lakes,
As they permeate.

The silent lion is the person-eater.

In the end will we manage our resources,
In the end will we be healthy,
In the end will we preserve the important things,

Confining the unconfined never works.

Milk and lakes; lakes and milk,
Become not like the waters of forgetfulness,
Permeable with weight,
Oh, dear! Milk and lakes.

April 3, 2016

39. The Classroom: Anywhere and Everywhere

If education is the key to success, where is the door?
How can we find it?
Search, learn, search, learn.

The classroom is a neutral environment,
Where the best of the best interact,
Search, teach, learn, cooperate.

It is within us to support each other,
It is surmountable to get to the next level,
We can each do it given the chance.

In the classroom we are given the lesson first,
Then the test follows,
Unfortunately, in life the tests are dished out,
Left, right, front, back, and center,
Then, if we are lucky, we learn the lesson.
We are still reeling in the lessons.
Versailles, Hiroshima, Vietnam, Afghanistan.

Human devastations are part of the lesson plan,
When will we fully learn?
In the classroom, whether under a tree,
In a high-tech plaza, or the neighborhood spot,
The inspiration is there, the ability to instill values,
Thoughtfulness, comprehension, and verity,
Verify the facts, double-check the method, meticulously.

Face value is not an option,
Double-check, triple-check,
Gravity is gravity, there is no way around it,
Energy and matter are neither created nor destroyed,
New knowledge and technology is fun,
Groundbreaking and breathtaking,
Is it success?

What is success? Success begets success,
With a safe, neutral, and conducive
Learning environment for all.

We learn the known knowns,
We challenge the known unknowns,
We discover the unknown unknowns. Good luck . . .

April 3, 2016

38. Cyclops Reflected

I see things!   My kind have
Do you see things?   Come and gone, but
Do you see them   Our work stays,
With any clarity   Our masters have
In any light?   Most of the say,
Oh, how I like   They mount, set, and
The perfect sight.   Release us for
It's a delight.   We must obey.

I shoot high and low,   For we snap and sway
I take aim fast or slow,   To our master's vision,
Black and white   With this lens
Extremely far and wide,   Interchangeably we
But shades of gray   Convey the news
Intervene with a stride.   And finish the mission.

I record hues of color   In the end we surrender
For my master,   To the light, our
My master takes me far and wide,   Blackness is complete. The inside
Places of seclusion,   of darkness is ours to
Nature, news, or disaster,   Keep, but the light, oh, the dear
Through many bumps of life side by side,   Light, it is measured and precise,
We seek action, commotion   And varies from sight to sight,
Still life and fame, plodding along   We imagine and open up,
The wildernesses until we tame.   Striving in search of the perfect sight.

April 9, 2016

37. The Truth Quest

"Who are you?"
She questioned me,
She cornered me,
She peppered and she pestered me.

She was tough,
She was no slouch.

She got hurt,
She had demands,
She grew tiresome,
She became.

She knew value,
She knew price.

She had deep insight,
She listened very well,
She had decorum and was kind,
She was inquisitively curious.

She kept confidences,
She was simply my anchor.

She was dependable as bedrock,
My guide in the civilized jungle,
My companion in stories and laughter,
My forever best friend.

February 25, 2016

36. Silly Saint Anger

Poor anger.
Anger is a tough proposition.

Anger is like a hot potato,
One must be prepared with gloves to ward off the heat,
Anger can come in many forms,
With the worst of all: a raging face full of puff and venom.

Reasonableness is displaced as ongoing anger creates
    hostility,
Who wants unpleasantness in a lovely home?
Who wants that in a productive environment?
Perhaps fools who can't tell the difference.
Or lunatics who pretend to know.

Anger is a waste of time and energy,
Albeit: there! We have it . . .
Energetic anguish that burns us within,
From the inside out: a boiling rage,
Garnishing our good hearts with hateful scars.

Anger presents unpleasantness by an ulcer or indigestion,
Indignation so vile it sears us before we can stop it,
Like abyss-peering: still waters run deep inside . . .
Pressing the right soul buttons, we may be ready to explode,
One more time, then another, and another again . . .

Boom, boom, bah . . . boom, boom, bah . . .

We're done. We are fools when we are angry,
Anger leaves scars just like a fence post,
All nailed down out of spite,
Then, with those nails removed, the glaring scars remain.

The divots, the craters, and the holes will never fully heal,
Because we succumbed to abyssal ignorance,
A sordid madness that could have been prevented,
The venom continues to fester and sear,
Is anger really worth it?

So, what is the true cost of anger?
What is the value of the position to always be right?
Oh, poor anger, what a plight!
Is it all relative? We must wonder . . .
How well we are undecided, fumble and blunder!

The absurdity of silly Saint Anger,
Continues with tremors long after the burst and shock . . .

March 12, 2016

35. White Room

My sanctity, my ideal space; my refuge, my quiet space,
Our home, not so much, maybe sometimes.
Perhaps the office, no way in hell!
Or the quiet library?
Better yet, being outdoors? No, too many bugs and
    mosquitoes.
Where then?

The inner sanctum rebuffs the harsh world,
With clean white walls and necessary orderliness,
Without clutter from out there,
Everything is in its rightful place, just so.

The cleanliness, the sweet magnolia aroma,
The much-relished comfort was planned to be all there,
At arm's length, at a moment's notice,
But alas, it was not meant to be.

The place on the bluff overlooking the Pacific,
With ethereal sunsets, the sensational breezes,
The unlimited drinks, the tasty, satiating food,
No, that dream never materialized.

Just spoken, just desired, just thought out loud,
Relished with plans made yet never implemented,
The white room.

The place where all the world's problems vanish,

The room where one can be safe, jolly, and carefree,
No more accentuated harsh lights, trivial questions,
Thorny bombardments, caustic remarks, nor acidic
     complaints.

Neutrality, no negatives,
The inner sanctum of peace buffered as with a surrounding
     moat,
The shield that protects us,
The sword that informs all to watch it.

It is within us. Is it there? No, just in here,
Did you find it? Did you find your center?
Did you know you have it? Keep on searching.
Know ourselves completely; if we fail, let's try again.

We are within ourselves, our own universe,
My center is mine, your center is yours,
If we join, we may create something unique,
We won't know until we try,
We must be willing to try again and again,
Let us try to find our white room together.

March 30, 2016

34. Perceptive Animals

Do you roll with the wolves?
Or stroll with the sheep?
You don't know?
Me neither . . .

We could be a sheep in wolf's skin,
Or a wolf covered with fluffy cotton wool,
It requires a certain skill to tell the difference,
The animals know, but do we?

Please sit down and learn,
In order to express our feelings,
Succinctly, correctly, appropriately,
Recall your courteous manners.

Not the right time,
Nor the right place,
Discretion, patience, and good timing,
We're not like animals.

It's still not like reading tea leaves,
It's a feeling of being true to ourselves,
It's a skill to let bygones be bygones,
It's a talent to let things go.

You ask me why? *Y* is a crooked letter,
Let it tumble in the wind,
Get chewed by the wolves,

Or get tangled in the fluffy wool.

Just be yourself,
Unique, perfect,
Ever changing, ever growing, ever moving,
Always at the center of the universe.

February 29, 2016

33. Sapphire: New Fashions

Tick, tock, tick, tock,
In with the new,
Tick, tock, tick, tock,
Out with the old.

Tick, tock, tick, tock,
Out with the new,
Tick, tock, tick, tock,
In with the old.

Styles change with time, reasons vary,
Perspective, wishfulness, or perception . . .
But principles? No . . . Values? No . . .
Honesty, integrity, and trustworthiness endure eternally.

Let's learn to unlearn
The things that don't work,
Let's learn to relearn
The things that make us better.

As far as style goes: I'm with you . . .
What's in nowadays?
You either are or you aren't?!
Shilly-shally blue shift or red shift? Azure, crimson, or
    grays?

Tick, tock, tick, tock,
Plum or sea . . . Which do you prefer to be?

Tick, tock, tick, tock,
Hope: skillfully whiz and become learned.

Tick, tock, tick, tock,
It's all relative,
Tick, tock, tick, tock,
We can learn, practice, and improve upon.

Time waits for nobody; the clock keeps ticking,
Success is never given, never guaranteed,
It's one step at a time akin to exceeding expectations,
But rather leveling to our natural wisdom and training.

February 29, 2016

32. On Stage

The world is a stage,
How do you dress yourself?
How you present yourself matters the most.

We were born and created for a purpose,
Some of us start early,
Others blossom and bloom late.

Expectations abound,
From parents, guardians, siblings, relatives, and friends.
For goodness' sake, even at work!
And the nameless, faceless society.

The grand stage has rules,
It's perilous, ruthless,
With harsh lights, one who shines during the day may burn
    you at night . . .
Stamina is key.

With a little bit of luck,
You won't get stuck,
With the special weapon: lots of elbow grease.

Help is on hand,
Despite the trapdoors,
Persons will help, lead, and direct,
Play along, listen up; enjoy yourself . . .

The costumes couple with scripted descriptive words,
All have meaning, a purpose,
Responsibly know their secrets and learn to play the role.

Interact, be willing to change,
Adapt, be flexing with a range,
Reflect, be thinking about the exchange.

When the play is done,
Just say, "Well played!
When will we play again?"

February 28, 2016

31. Metamorphosis

Two peas in a pod,
No, the caterpillars,
Eat, eat, eat; for what?

Save, save, save,
Be, be, be,
Live, live, live,
Indeed, for what?

Let's stay together,
Let the outside world toil itself away and go by,
Avoid bringing home troubles,
Leave them at the door.

Stay with me,
Just us,
Just here,
Right now, rest and relax.

Okay, we're in the cocoon,
Now what?
Just stay,
Just land and stay.

You and me,
Then we shall see.
This is our white room where we are carefree.

February 28, 2016

30. Our Auric Moment

We left Mendocino early,
Driving south from the Irish Coast,
We had lunch in Bodega Bay.

With a brash promise said I,
"Honey, sunset at the Golden Gate Bridge."
She said, "Yeah, right." Typical.
The traffic meandered along the Pacific Coast Highway.

PCH licked the coast,
We kept trekking and driving,
I got lost,
I got stuck in traffic.

Marin County was in shadow,
I started to say, "Why did I make such a promise?"
We inched along very slowly,
I could see the golden signs.

We crept some more, and then,
I drove at posted speeds,
As the expanse of the bay opened up,
A glorious sun on the horizon.

Quivering, fading, and saying good-bye to that day,
She stared and she smiled intensely,
I continued driving, slowing down to peer at the sunset,
With both hands on the wheel.

Finally, she turned around and said to me,
"The little hairs on your hands are golden.
Thank you for such a magical moment."

February 28, 2016

29. Unavoidable Signs

Suddenly, in an instant, we know life can change,
We keep missing the signs, so pay attention!

In October, I was rear-ended in a car accident,
I escaped him and walked away unscathed.
Mr. Death looked over his shoulder and winked,
He warned me, "Slow down. Easy does it, patience!"

On New Year's Eve, we witnessed a fellow diner
At a fancy restaurant suffer,
Nearly choking to death,
On a piece of meat too big to swallow,
Mrs. Death was closer, she sashayed and wiggled away.

That night I told her, "Happy New Year, my love,
Please do not worry; I dedicate everything to you,
You are my whole world,
Everything that is mine is yours,
Everything I do, I do for you."

2016 . . . Ready or not: here we come,
The third rock, tumbling and tossing in space,
By and by, the New Year was here.
Throughout January, she talked about
All her relatives, friends, and people she knew.

Bloody Death was whispering in her ear,
He got his grip on her; he's so easygoing and smooth.

She spoke of dead people we both knew:
Arden, Shari, Charlotte, Bill Aaron,
Some I did not know well: her parents,
Her longtime friends.

Mrs. Death, she's too cunning and caught her well,
In February, she was gone too soon.
Mr. and Mrs. Death, we have played five times,
Next time: when sent for me—I'm ready, when you're ready.

Rest in peace, my love, for now I am carrying on,
Until then, every day is a gift, and I wish to live the fullest.

February 28, 2016

28. Hairy Brains

Possessed by all, most useful to a few.

Good persons share, bad people tell,
Good persons love, bad people hate,
Is it that simple?

Well: maybe, yes; maybe, no,
What did you say?

It depends, persons have reasons as to how they feel,
Certain aspects, certain views,
Globally experienced.

Okay, then.
Do we just be or be done?
That depends: easier said than done.
On what, wise one?
Um, where shall we begin . . .

Our history,
Specifically, our heritage,
Patience and perseverance will do wonders.

Our nation's culture,
Our past relationships with others,
Our limited knowledge,
Our preconceived ideas,
Our communication process.

Our heroes communicated well,
They left us great stories to follow.

So there's no hope?
Well, hope is everything, even if false.
We can learn to create a better destiny.

That's found between our ears.

February 25, 2016

27. The Essential Onion

Bermuda, Vidalia, red, pearl, garlic, or shallots?
Non, non, non, non!
Don't you have enough for the soup?
Non, non, non, non,
Chop, chop, sniffle, sniffle.

Pourquoi?
Why, why, why, why do you ask?
Remember, I'm the one with the knife!
If you insist,
Chop, chop, sniffle, sniffle.

The pungent aroma surrounds us,
The sautéed onion gives flavor,
The translucent effect so sweet,
The crunchiness dramatic,
The burnt texture light and empowering.

The onion, a powerful ingredient to master,
Just like persons as the levels spiral away,
Deep, deep, down the center to the core,
Yes, the outside is easily seen, with not enough smell to
     sense,
Just as simple as one appears to be.

But what lives behind those dazzling green eyes?
What's twitching behind those luscious choc-brown eyes?
What's tingling behind these gorgeous azure-blue eyes?

Oh, I'm dying to know . . .
Really, really . . .

Well, hold yourself because one should be careful,
You asked: just like the pungent smell of the onion,
Persons offer a scent, some attract and some repel,
Are you sure? Are you ready?
Please do not get anxious.

Brace yourself because you are in for a heck of a ride!
Just like the roller coaster, I will whiz you away,
You will lose your breath and will want to stay,
Time is fleeting, and when the ride is done,
We start chopping all over again before we had barely begun.

March 16, 2016

26. Our Unique Faces

A pleasant smile, a knowing wink,
The quivering lip, and the well-defined eyebrow.

Our faces are our own,
A perfection of our souls,
A constant motion of emotions,
Balanced with bones, tense muscles, supple skin, and
    hairline.

We are responsible for our faces,
For what comes out of our mouths,
For what we put in our mouths, too,
The glorious gift of life shows up on our faces.

A precious trust,
A mutual give and take,
Make or break,
Help or harm.

It's in our faces,
It's what we see when we look in the mirror,
Will we truly recognize ourselves through life's phases?
What have we done? The choice in remembering is ours . . .

The good and the bad,
Are we keeping track of what makes us glad?
Somber not; it's in the look, the gaze.

Her high cheekbones, his bushy mustache,
Her vibrant eyes, his strong chin,
Her curly eyelashes, his well-kept beard,
Her simple freckles, his cute dimple.

The face with a dead giveaway,
Her tilt of the head just so, his twitching jawline,
The tell of a poker face is there to be discovered.

Only once, only one, for an esteemed someone.
A special person,
It's our own, a truly distinct and distinguished feature,
The look, the feel, and the style.

So carry on, stand tall, and face the world,
Accept and embrace most, if not all, and keep on smiling . . .

March 27, 2016

25. Jewel Tomfoolery

Aren't we good enough?
Aren't the good things in life good enough?
Why do we slaughter and persecute others?
Why do we malign children with hatred?
Why do we keep unnecessary tensions so high?

We can't all be like Uncle Tom?
Nor can we all be Mrs. Jewel?
Why do we keep to silence as such atrocities prevail?
Why do we laugh like hyenas at such disgusting things?

Oh! Yes, it's not my problem,
Oh! Yes, it's all business,
Oh! Yes, because I was ordered to do so,
Oh! Yes, it is the way we have always done it.

Indeed, indeed, one soul to another,
Indeed, indeed, one eye for an eye,
Indeed, indeed, turn a blind eye,
Indeed, indeed, just do nothing until it's your turn.

Yes, life is hard and life is challenging,
Yes, life requires sacrifice and choices,
No, living does not require hurting others,
No, living does not create the hardships we crave.

Life is precious, life can be kinder,
We can do better,

By helping each other,
United collectively just like the bees.

Cooperate, mitigate, coordinate,
Buzz along with auspiciousness,
Deliver the honey,
Nothing needs to be skewed.

Minding our own business, depending on ourselves,
If provoked, we defend ourselves!
But most important: make the sweet honey.
Buzzing around, tending to the pollen and flowers,
Without harming others but rather helping one another.

March 17, 2016

24. Accidental Vignettes

It only happened once, I swear, I didn't mean it,
It happened only once, you say?
How about the consequences?
Is it eighteen years or just a few days?

It happened again and again,
Repeat and repeat the same behaviors,
Expecting different results.
We cannot continue to do this, that, and the other,
We must stop to examine and reexamine our behaviors.

It happened so suddenly, my, oh, my,
How the road to hell is paved with good intentions,
Intentions so elegantly put,
So intensely explained, so convincingly displayed.

It happened more than once,
Well, let's learn from our past mistakes,
So we can give a wide berth,
Avoidance is a great skill,
It may even give you freedom and a thrill.

It can only happen once,
Just like the gazelle leaping in the air to avoid fatality,
By making sure it will survive to see another day,
For the next day, surely, it will run faster and faster,
Keeping a keen eye on the ever-present cheetah.

It happened so swiftly,
What were you thinking? Never mind, you weren't,
Did you not consider all the facts? All the risks?
Yet, you bumble along with wishful thinking or
    pie-in-the-sky ideas.

It can happen again and at any time,
Keep your distance from the perils, stay vigilant and alert,
Use the foliage to shield you, remain attentive and ever
    ready,
Just like the brave firefighters,
Who, at a moment's notice, rush into burning buildings.

It was an accident, you say, huh, next time be ever so careful,
Ever so, weigh the outcomes before you put others at risk,
Because stupid actions or inactions are not an option,
We should know better by now.

March 16, 2016

23. Witness with Cadence

It's story time! Let the story unfold,
Try not to be bold.

Don't ask her her age, or how much money she makes,
Nor comment negatively on her appearance or weight,
Nor the color of her hair.

Let things unfold,
Compliment her, respect her,
Gradually, haphazardly,
Things unfold some more.

Care for her,
Qualm her not,
Give her unconditional love.

It's a joyful journey,
More fun with no ultimatums,
No must do's,
Enjoy now while it lasts, it's all we have,
When you're ready, I'm ready . . .

She will start to share
The important things in her life,
So listen up, write it down.

Slowly, easy does it, gather up the things she loves,
Bring and offer them to her,

Surprise her, spoil her, cherish her,
So that she can spoil and cherish you, too.

Be ready, be prepared . . .
In her own time, in her own way,
She will convey, she will give, and she will share.

Patience now, you do not want to miss it,
Only when she's ready . . .

February 29, 2016

22. The Barber's Place

Snip, snip, clippers and scissors,
Clip, clip, razors and combs,
Tuck, tuck, brushes and towels,
Clean, clean, looking sharp, spic and span.

Back in ancient Egypt, the high priest paid respects,
To the neighborhood barber.
Indeed, indeed: who whizzed off the wild.

Our guys are on it,
They listen, they laugh,
They smile with their eyes on the mark,
Their hands steady with the flow.

Clearly: not easy come, easy go.

Always taking care of his customers,
My barber is someone to know, my go-to person,
Always ready to take care of me.

Barbers know the drill,
They know the dance,
Easily ebb and flow . . .
A distinction of class, a cut above.

A prestige that is sacred and divine,
Well done,
My friend, thanks for taking care of us.

March 14, 2016

21. SS *Marmoreal Dreams*

Marble is heavy and sinks,
Why that name?
Even for your fishing boat?
Won't it sink in open water?
With or without a catch?

No, it's a dream,
Yes, it is my dream,
Okay, how will you make it happen?

First of all, I'm keeping my day job,
After work, in the other eight hours,
I will tinker and toil,
Design and construct,
Search for better ideas to make it happen.

And what about your wasted time?
What wasted time? Please . . .
It's a joy to pursue dreams.

Dreams are the stuff we live for,
Just like the essentials of happiness,
Someone to live with and love, something purposefully worthy,
Something to hope and yearn for,
What more can we ask for in this life? That's enough and will do.

March 1, 2016

20. Yes, Dear

Take out the trash; yes, dear,
Bring in the groceries; yes, dear.

Pick up the laundry; yes, dear,
Help me with the door; yes, dear,
Did you do this and that? Yes, dear,
Okay, well, let's get a move on; yes, dear.

Did you feed the kids? Yes, dear,
Did you bathe the kids? Yes, dear.
All in all, I'm here for you, dear,
Through thick and thin, we're united together.

It's our life together, our story,
Our triumphs, our challenges, and our way of being.

Yes, dear; yes, dear,
Can change to: no, dear,
No, thank you, dear,
Not today, dear.

Most interesting, though, is that a person smiles,
Inside and out,
At how our significant other handles things and issues,
Especially when the other admits to making a mistake.

All along, inside saying without imposing,
There's another way to do this or that,

But you just have to ask me.
Yes, dear; yes, dear.
What would you like to do this weekend?
Anything that will please you, dear.

How about Friday dinner?
Whatever you desire, dear.
Tacos, salad, roast chicken, barbeque,
Oh, yes, dear.

Creating harmony is the key
To living at ease with your soul mate and companion.

February 29, 2016

19. Herr *und* Frau Befragen: Questions

Here, there, or over there?
Did you find out all you needed?
Do you know all the facts?
How does your gut feel?

Your brain says yes. How about your heart?
Wait a minute.
Stop.
Take a break.

Will this decision have an impact ten years from today?
If yes, wait—ponder some more.
If no, get on with it.
Stop wasting time.

Mistakes are mistakes.
The more we make, the better the economy.
The more we learn, the smarter we are.
However, repeating the mistake is like insanity,
That is to expect different results from the same effort.

Different energy levels
Create different problems,
Which cycle into different solutions.
Influencer: Did we ask the right questions? Asking is not
    stupidity.

The last question to ask:
Am I part of the problem or the solution?

Your choice, your answer,
Your decision, so face the consequences.

February 24, 2016

18. Granular Ideas

I have an idea!
Eureka!
Dear child, what is your idea?

Well, I'm playing at the beach,
Yes, child.
I like it here,
Go on.

I'm at the beach,
And I have an idea,
Okay, what's your idea?

My sand castle is big,
Help me, please,
Yes, precious.

More sand here, more sand there,
Oops, no more here,
Yes, child,
We're at the beach.

Dear child,
I wish you to grow with brilliant ideas,
As parents and guardians: we wish you all the best!

February 23, 2016

17. In Conjunction with Rich Rules and Permissions

Whence do we start?

Yours, mine, or ours? Theirs?
Did we agree to this?
No, wait! What just happened?
How did we miss this?

Change is inevitable,
Even the crow knows,
Cawing and cackling,
Even the vulture sees,
Swarming, buzzing, and diving.

Also, the trending sunflower
Follows the sun,
The brilliant moonflower
Opens up with the moon.

When did we get so lost?
The rule, the exception,
The change to the rule,
The change to the exception to the rule,
Consequently, the exception to the exception to the rule.

Really? Not so simple and straightforward, huh!

February 23, 2016

16. Expectations of Relationships

Easy or tough,
Sweet or sour,
Pleasant or ugly,
Divine and clean,
Yes, to all of the above and more.

People are all carbon,
Some are messy like charcoal,
Others smear like oily graphite,
A few cut deeply like diamond.

We're made out of tough stuff,
Like Livingstone,
Like Washington,
We can get it done,
We can see things through to the end.

No person is an island,
But a link in a network,
Like a spider's web,
Sticky and tricky.

We have to willingly learn how to weave our way,
Adapt ourselves gracefully,
Seek necessity with forgiveness,
Mostly, by always doing our very best.

February 22, 2016

15. Fence

On a hot summer's day,
We purchased the lumber,
We loaded his truck,
I jumped in and sat shotgun.

Astonished and amazed,
He said, "What are you doing?"
I said, "We're riding in your truck together."
"No, you're not, get in your car."
"Oh, ow," I bellowed like a cow.
Sheepishly, I jumped out.

We soon got to work,
Erected the smallest nifty fence,
Afterward, we heartily ate a good dinner,
By and by, the planted roses grew,
A hobby was born,
A friendship solidified.

With years going by, we laugh a lot,
At the shotgun stance,
The moo-ish sound,
With the accomplishment abound.

February 23, 2016

14. Food for Thought

What's changed?
Is the food tasty?
Too salty?
Oh, my dear.

Have a sip of water,
Wipe your lips,
How about a sweet dessert?
Oh, my dear.

What would you like to do next?
Relax a bit,
Let's talk,
What's changed?

Is there another?
Who, what, when, where?
Oh, no, my dear.
Why, my dear?

February 23, 2016

13. Embracing Challenges: Fear Not

Don't give me a blade,
Even when I cry for it,
Don't give me heat,
Even when I'm cold.

Don't give me chili,
Even when I ask for it,
Don't infect me,
Even when you have it.

Don't give me life,
Even if you cannot,
But you have no choice in the matter,
Whether you like it or not.

I will cut myself,
Will burn,
Will taste bad things,
Will be sick.

This is life,
Our lives are full of problems.
Problems are here,
Our problems will be overcome, nonetheless.

February 23, 2016

12. Shekha: Her Mouth

I saw her recently,
It wasn't her,
So similar, so alike, but what distinct feature?

I stopped what I was saying,
I glanced back and did a double take.

It was her mouth.
The shape was so similar to hers.

I remembered her laughter,
And her kind smile.

She was that sweet,
Wholehearted.

We love you, dear graceful one,
We miss you,
We'll see you in heaven.

February 22, 2016

11. Seif: His Strength

Boy wanted on your team for any game,

He was a nimble player,
He was strong,
He had a contagious laugh.

He taught me how to ride a bicycle,
He laughed at me when I fell down and bruised my eye.

Boy became man, grew taller,
Grew up stronger,
We never met as we got older,
Our paths never crossed again.

Those days are long gone,
He became frail with illness.

We will meet in heaven,
For now, rest in peace,
We'll remember him always,

As strong and solid, Seif.

February 22, 2016

10. Folding Sheets Well

Her touch was firm yet elegant,
Her instructions were simple and straightforward,

We were in the laundry room,
In the Bronx,
Folding king-size sheets.

I did not know how to do it.
She taught me well.

Every time I make the bed,
I remember her instructions well,
Start here, tug there,
Sharp, crisp corners.

It is the bed you sleep in,
Respect it,
In turn, you will rest well.

Thank you, dearest
Cousin.

February 21, 2016

9. Moments in Life

Swiftly, fast,
With no blessing,
Time can sink by,
Just like the sun over the horizon.

We cannot hold it,
Nor can we keep it,
Just passes by.

Special moments are different,
Just like the colors within the spectra of a prism,
Iridescent, vibrant, and memorable,
The eye recognizes nature's beauty.

In a day, how many will you see?
Remember beauty is in the eye of the beholder,
So every time you meet someone,
Wish them well.

Gaze closely into his or her eyes,
Wonder a little,
Ask: Has she or he seen anything beautiful recently?
If so, what was it?

Who was it?
When was it?
Share the experiences that are important to you,
You get to bring them alive every time.

February 21, 2016

8. Going Grocery Shopping

The day is here, yea!
Or nay?
What's on the weekly menu?
What's on my list?

Focus, focus: do not yield to candy temptation.
The cart or handbasket?
Well, the cart makes it easier to load everything,
But checking out is painful.
The handbasket is heavier,
But reminds me of necessity.

Open mouth, lick my lips,
All the good food,
All the junk food,
At my reach: choose wisely.

Focus, focus diligently: wait, hold on, no candy.
Healthy food.
Will we eat all that?
Too much, too little.

Guess what: we'll just have to come back another time.
We have enough for now.

February 21, 2016

7. Galvanismo Electricity

Drip, drop, drip, drop,
Is it full yet?

Days drip into weeks,
And weeks pour into months,
And they in turn gush into years . . .
As the decades gather momentum and flow,
We become one,
We become us.

None of your positive reassurances,
Kind and small gestures of affection, are missed,
None are taken for granted as our anniversary reappears,
It is the day the drips began, drip, drip.

They continue to flow, and I am truly much more in awe,
Of you, of us, and how we have solidified our love,
By dedicating and aligning our souls,
To one another and for each other.

Thank you for giving me the chance, the trust, the affection,
The care a man can only dream of.
When the going gets tough, let us remind one another of
    our humble, magical, and electrifying beginning.

With all my love: now and forever.

February 21, 2016

6. Numbers: Two Three Two One

Two steps forward,
Three steps backward,
Two steps to the right,
One step to the left,
Where are you now?

Which way did you go?
Are you completely lost?
Star searching up high?
Do you know where you are?

Two Three Two One
It's Eight.
Still lost?

Well, before embarking,
Make sure you know,
Where you are going,
Your purse strings waist-side,
You may get help along the way,
Or you may be eaten along the way.

The rabbit is smart,
But don't discount the tortoise,
They both travel,
Two Three Two One . . .

February 19, 2016

5. Flawless Time

Reflect: Are you thinking and regretting with time?
Have you forgotten where we came from?
What are you doing with your time here?
Are you remembering us with your prayers?

The world never ends or stops,
People are chasing and looking,
For things and position,
Fooled, indeed.

Pause a little,
Stand here,
Look,
Observe.

Sit on the bank of the river,
The river snakes slowly,
The water creates its own path,
It starts in the mountains,
Ends in the ocean,
Evaporates in the hot sun,
Moving just like fluffy cotton, it rains again in the
    mountains.

We go around, down, up,
Up, down,
Right, left,
The same place we return.

Time waits for no person,
Time can be poor and generous,
The timing is everything,
By having the time of one's life.

February 17, 2016

4. Bare Parents

If my Mother is a mother,
Even if she's a cart,
Then who is Dad?
Or Grandma, Grandpa, Uncle, and Auntie, too?

Our guardians have raised us well,
It takes a village to look after and nurture us,
All of our children.

One does this,
And the other does that,
We do not know everything about living,
We pray to Our Dear Lord every day.

Now let's get along with each other,
Be cautious with our behavior,
Self-discipline is important,
Respect is paramount and patience helps.

However, once you reach your wit's end,
Say, "Thank you for your help,
I will carry my own load,
And proceed forward in life's journey."

"I know you wish me the very best,
Also, I wish you the very best,
Let's willingly help one another again."

February 17, 2016

3. Transcendental Music

Tell me, what's your favorite beat?
A little bit of taarab*?
Lots of jazz?
Or the blues?

Let's shake and dance,
Let's play together,
I'll change the beat,
Let's try reggae,
You don't like to bounce, you don't like it . . .

Let's slow things down,
Romantic love songs are playing,
Come closer,
Feel me,
Let's hold each other completely,
Now, kiss me, please . . .

February 16, 2016

Taarab is a mixture of music styles influenced by traditional Arabic, Indian, European, and Zanzibari musical forms found in East Africa. A similar trend developed in Puerto Rico and became the worldwide salsa dance movement.

2. My Family

Me, you, us; them, too?
Where do we start? With Grandpa or his?
Why are we forgetting Grandma and hers?
Wives and husbands, their children, how are they living?
They live one day at a time.

However, others say a small family is better,
Just Mom, Dad, and their kids,
What about Uncle, Aunt, Grandma, and Grandpa, where are
    they?
And our other relatives, too?

It is true life is full of challenges with problems,
Problems will come and go,
Our relatives will come and go, too,
Remember there is nothing new or free.

Persons require attention,
Pay close attention to those around us,
Help them if you can,
Listen to them if you can,
Do your very best if you can.

By helping each other, we give the gift of life to one another,
By being there, it's much more than right or wrong,
By being here, we witness each other's lives unfold.

February 15, 2016

1. My Ardent Love

Where are you?
All these days, where have they gone?
When will you come back?
I'm here waiting for you, but you're not here,
I do not know what to do now.

If I call you, you're not there,
If I send you a letter, you never reply,
If I look at your pictures, I cannot hear your sweet voice.

It's true, you have left me,
I will never see you again,
I will never hear your sweet voice,
I will never touch your body.

Oh, My Dear Lord, please let me see you in heaven,
I will try to do my very best,
I will attempt to do good things with all my strength and
     effort,
I want you; only you.

Your soul is resting now, and I will see you,
One day, two days, three days,
A month or two,
If it's not like that,
Then let it be years as I am here just for you.

Valentine's Day, February 14, 2016

Acknowledgments

The Attitude of Gratitude

Asiyefunzwa . . . hufunzwa na Uliwmengu . . . The one not taught . . . is schooled by the Universe . . .

(Swahili saying)

If an ounce of caution is worth a pound of cure, what is gratitude worth? "Thanks a million" is a phrase I use daily. Thank you for taking the time to visit my website, supporting my work, and giving me invaluable feedback.

This journey we call life and living has given me the opportunity to interact with so many good persons. I am grateful for these chance encounters. There are so many persons I have to thank. The numbers must be in the thousands. Our lives are filled with luck. In my mind luck means ***Love Unconditionally with Courtesy and Kindness.*** You may notice this line in one of the poems.

We live in a continuum of yeses and noes. Subsequently, the choices, interactions, and unintended consequences take over: fate, happenstance, or good fortune. That one cold day in March, I made a simple left turn instead of a right turn on Woodward Avenue in Detroit, Michigan, with no map or cell phone and kept driving. I got thoroughly lost and absorbed everything as I drove. Determined with an inkling of new experiences, a willingness to explore and discover led me to my sweetheart. A simple application led me to a whole new world and lifestyle. If we choose to, we can trace this myriad of choices that culminate in the fabric of living.

Please consider the following scenario and assumptions. Then, perhaps, we can earnestly answer this question: *Are we not a happy, lucky bunch?* The gift of life is recognizing all the beautiful souls we encounter in our short lives. Now, as a practicing mathemagician (I love mathematics and numbers), here are some numbers. Assume the simple work timeline: 15 years with 50 workweeks comprising 5 days during the week will result in a figure of 3,750 working days or 30,000 working hours.

Conservatively, consider that each one of us interacted with about 30,000 persons and made *at least one person* smile or laugh in each *hour of work*. You be the judge. Radiantly, let us laugh and smile with one another with no expectations in return: a fairly simple mutual exchange will brighten our days as we create the *Smile Brigade*.

My hope and goal is to share my life experiences with you. My observations of life are unique but common. My desire is to question our decisions by reviewing, remembering, and tracing the choices of our actions and/or inactions. Our Swahili culture is universally rich with timeless proverbs, parables, sayings, and virtues. We are constantly reminded of the good things in life. A fundamental lesson is about becoming who we are meant to be.

My ultimate goal is best described by legendary race car driver Lyn St. James in the book *Oh, By the Way (A letter from my mother)*. These are Lyn's words: "Pearls of wisdom that are given and valued should be shared. I want to share this letter from my mother with you and I hope you'll share it with your loved ones." Our desire is that you will also share the gift of the Swahili culture with your loved ones, too. Swahili hope helps all.

For those we love and cherish; for the one who ardently guides and shares her or his *luck* coupled with hope at times when we need it the most. It takes one to reach one; it takes one to teach one.

With much love and appreciation: thank you very much indeed!

Alin

About the Author

Alinuru Yasin began writing poetry as a child while attending boarding school in England and South Africa. The Swahili riddles and proverbs he learned in his native Tanzania continue to influence his life. His passion for connecting through shared cultural experiences has taken him on travels around the globe. Before immigrating to the United States in 2000, he was an African safari guide and later became a cultural representative. He currently lives in Michigan with his two Yorkshire terriers. *Good Grief: Sixty Days with Sixty Poems* is his first book of poetry.

Made in the USA
Middletown, DE
30 July 2017